God Cannot Lie is printed by CreateSpace
(an amazon.com company) and is available at
amazon.com and other retail outlets.

GOD CANNOT LIE

Each scripture reference used in this book is noted with the abbreviation of the version used. The notations are as follows:

AMP: Amplified Bible
AMPC: Amplified Bible, Classic Edition
ASV: American Standard Version
KJV: King James Version
NASB: New American Standard Bible
NIV: New International Version
NKJV: New King James Version
NLT: New Living Translation

GOD CANNOT LIE

FORWARD

This young woman, Rhonda Spencer, has written this wonderful book that will inspire everyone who reads it. She doesn't receive the report of the doctor, she receives the report of the Lord. She will not be denied what God's word says.

She knows God Cannot Lie because His word says in John 14:14, "If you shall ask anything in my name, I will do it!" Rhonda just stood on the Word regardless of what friends, family or doctors said. As Rhonda continued to stand, the manifestations of her prayers were answered.

Come and go on this exciting journey as you read this book. Be ready for your faith level to rise and increase, and the zeal of God to consume you. As you read this book there will be many people that God will quicken to you who need to read this book. If God heard Rhonda's prayers, he will also hear yours. Use the principle she said she used:
Hebrews 11:6 "but without faith it is impossible to please Him; for he that cometh to God must believe He is, and He is a rewarder of those that diligently seek Him."

~*Patricia Avanzini*

MIRACLES STILL HAPPEN

12 September 2016, the day after one of the largest events that our church organizes, after experiencing sickness and weakness in my body for the past 6-8 months, I went to see the doctor for testing. Those 6-8 months had been horrific. In the beginning my husband had no idea what was going on, and I did not want to tell him. After being unable to get out of bed, I knew I could no longer hide or fight on my own. Before long the words "we suspect cancer" came out of the very kind and educated doctor standing before me. Without even a pause I responded, "It is all right. I have already gotten down on my knees and prayed to God, and I know that I am healed." I had not planned on saying any of that, but it came out of me with a force. As we both heard the words coming from my mouth, I was sure she thought I was completely crazy.

It was at this point that my husband and I determined to not tell people about the diagnosis and certainly not give the devil any glory for his hideous actions.

We were determined that the only glory we would give would glorify God.

I began to saturate myself with the hearing of the Word of God, increasing my faith, watching miracle videos on YouTube and getting in the presence of God on a constant basis.

The severity of the diagnosis began a deluge of testing. I was in and out of the hospital every few days with more needles, blood work, MRIs, CAT scans, a pet scan was scheduled, sedations, biopsies and terribly ugly bruises. When the call came that the doctor was requesting to see me the next morning at 7:30AM, it was completely unexpected because I knew I was healed. The question came to mind, "Why he would want to see me so early?"; this got me thinking that it must be urgent. And just like that - fear began to creep in attempting to take the place of my faith.

As the experienced doctor, who was well respected as a knowledgable medical professional in his field, revealed that the biopsy reports confirmed cancer, I once again firmly stood my ground. I looked him in the eye, genuinely thanked him for his information but kindly informed him, as I did to the previous doctor, "I am healed."

NOW I HAD TO STAND and when I had done all to stand, keep standing.

I did not receive the report that there was nothing there. But why? Over my years of ministry, I had prayed with so many who were facing questionable scans themselves; I had rejoiced with them when the scans came back negative. I expected the very same result for myself: that they would find nothing there.

So for the first time, for real, I had to check my own faith.

Faith is only a theory, until you have to use it!

This is where "fighting the good fight of faith" comes into play. Immediately, my mind went to questioning:
"Do I have sin in my life?"
"Why is this happening to me?"
"Will I not be healed?"
"Am I going to die?"

There were times when the tears would well up in my eyes and other times they would just flow. Then there were the times when the doctor's words would replay over and over in my mind while an overwhelming fear gripped me, taking my breath away. But, I fought the pity party Satan was throwing in my face. I declared, "SATAN WILL GET NO GLORY FROM ME."

Then I was swept right into meetings with various doctors, all telling me what they were going to do and how they desired to immediately begin radiation and chemotherapy five days a week; staging the cancer based on their best knowledge. I looked at one of the doctors, who is considered "the best" in his field, and stopped him from continuing with telling me his treatment plan. Instead I began to tell him what I had told the others. "I believe that I am healed."

With all of the professionalism of what this physician does each day, he looked at me and said, "I am sorry, but once cancer is diagnosed, that is what it is no matter how much you do not want it to be." I thanked him and told him that I would begin whatever treatment plan he thought would be best, but only after he conducted a re-biopsy because, again, I knew I was healed. I want to be transparent with you as you read this: even as I said it boldly with my mouth, I was fighting the doubt and fear loudly shouting on the inside of me where nobody could hear it. He agreed to do it again in the next round of testing, but only to "prove" me wrong.

From that very first moment, I had completely saturated myself morning and night with the **TRUTH OF GOD'S WORD.** I needed God's life-giving Word to be greater and more lifted up than any of the words spoken, and greater than the thoughts and fears attempting to take my mind hostage.

I needed Truth to trump my facts.

I did not have the luxury to be complacent. No one else's faith will work for me...
"Woman ***your faith*** has made you whole."

I was presented with life and death; with the decision to believe, or not believe, that TRUTH TRUMPS FACTS. And with all the religious junk in my head, gut theologies deep within me, my subconscious was battling with THE TRUTH THAT TRUMPS FACTS. I had an onslaught of them to get through: I had to ONLY BELIEVE.

Have faith in God. Trust that all His promises are true and that GOD CANNOT LIE.

I sat in a tiny, cold, metallic treatment room listening to the doctor speaking his diagnosis, "cancer", and rattling off his plan for treatment. Then, hearing words I never thought I would hear spoken to me...my heart welled up with compassion for others who every day sit in that same chair, but don't know Jesus and have no hope. How many before me had to sit in that same chair only to feel despair? I cannot imagine not having hope in the power of God to heal **all** pains and disease.

The doctor agreed to one last test before starting treatment, scheduled for only around 10 days later. Even though every test that had been performed showed cancer (confirmed by the board of doctors at the Mayo Clinic) even into the lymph nodes, I stood on my sure belief that Christ is the great healer. If He did it for one, He would do it for me. He is no respecter of persons. He is the same yesterday, today and forever.

I stood firm and fixed on the truth that:
GOD CANNOT LIE!

Then the news came. I got a call from the Doctor himself. They did many biopsies in that last test, and they could find "no cancer."

NO CANCER WAS FOUND!

From that moment every breath in my lungs has taken on new meaning and appreciation.

I was healed just as I had declared, and fought to remain in faith for, from the first of many doctors appointments.

I am healed!

Have you ever seen a miracle with your own eyes? Have you seen proof that God still heals today? I am so happy to be able to glorify God alone and share picture proof of a *today* miracle.

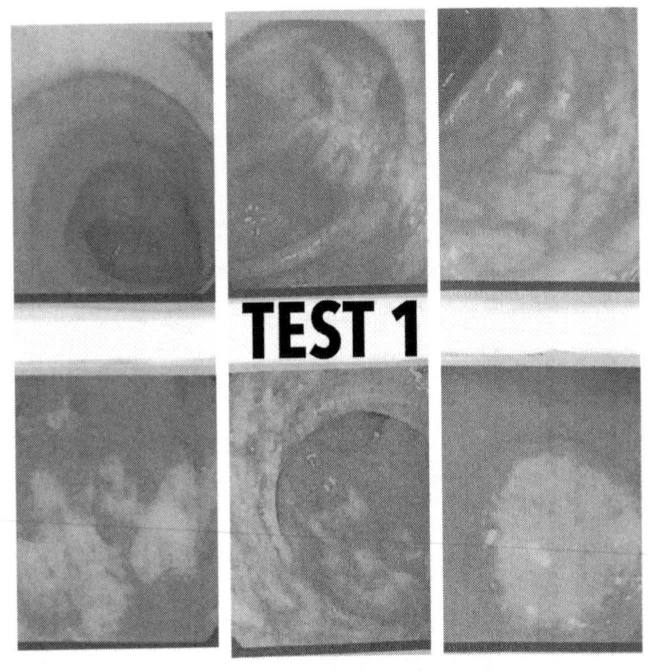

Here, in Test 1, you can see the white circle spot of cancer, confirmed by a board of doctors at the Mayo clinic. Next is the actual letterhead with my hospital, my name and their report of Test 1.

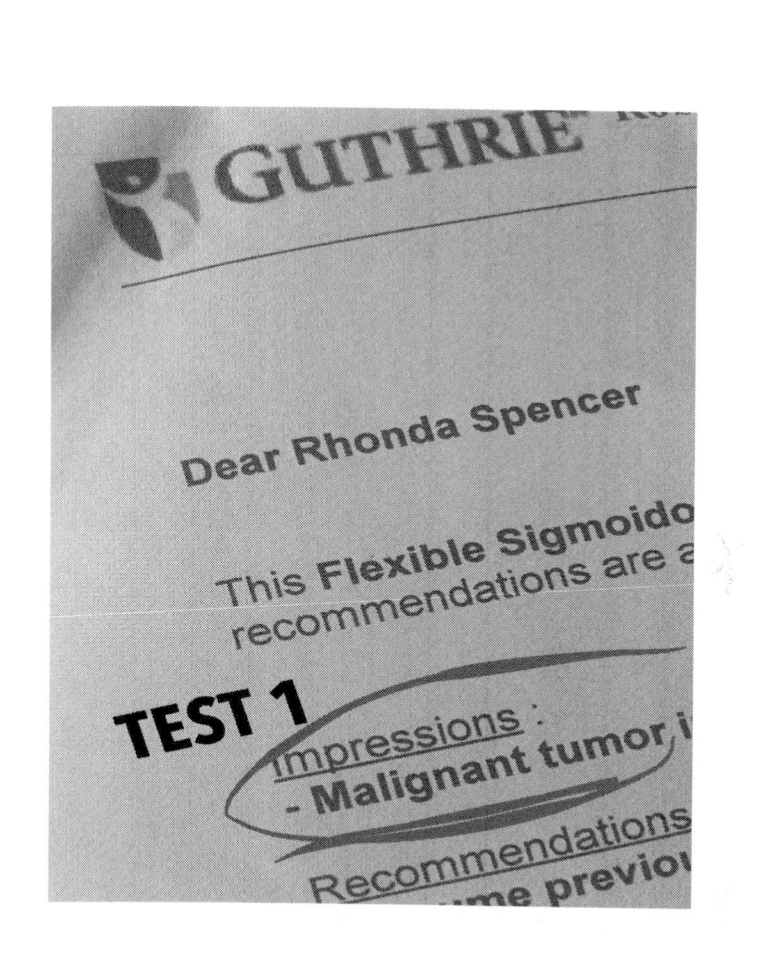
GUTHRIE
Dear Rhonda Spencer
This Flexible Sigmoido
recommendations are
TEST 1
Impressions :
- Malignant tumor
Recommendations

Here is Test 2, where they tattooed the white circle spot of cancer with it's staging results in the letter just below it.

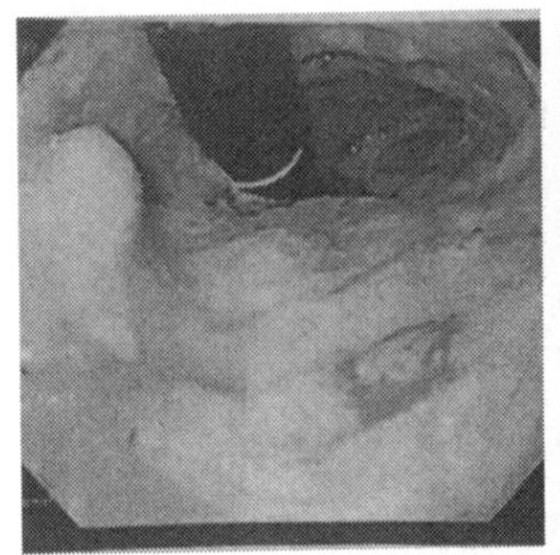

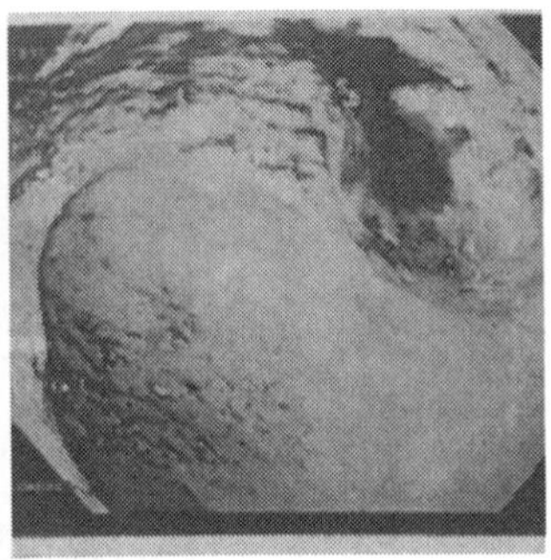

TEST 2

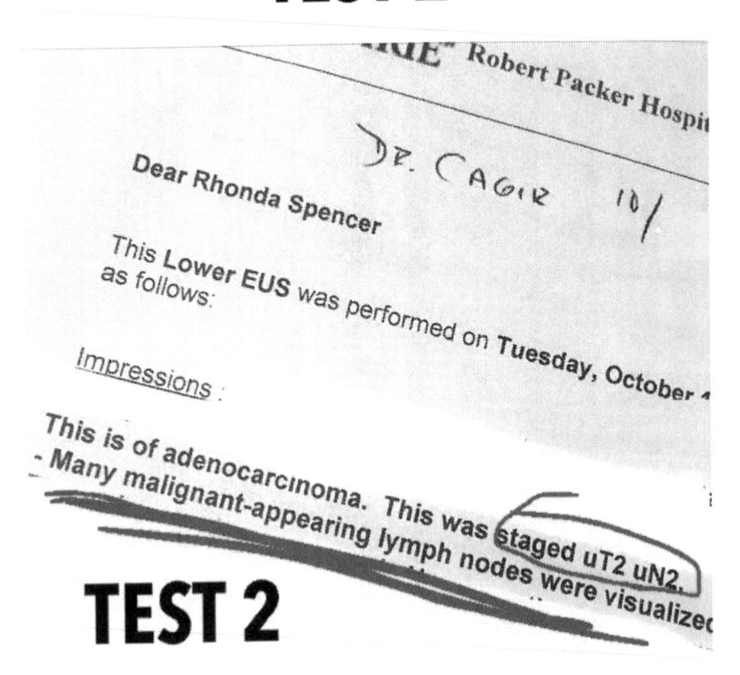

Robert Packer Hospi

Dr. Cagir 10/

Dear Rhonda Spencer

This **Lower EUS** was performed on **Tuesday, October** as follows:

Impressions :

This is of adenocarcinoma. This was staged uT2 uN2.
- Many malignant-appearing lymph nodes were visualized

TEST 2

Then, just a few days later, the third and final visual test was performed. Look at the almost new looking skin compared to the first two, and then the written proof results that follow.

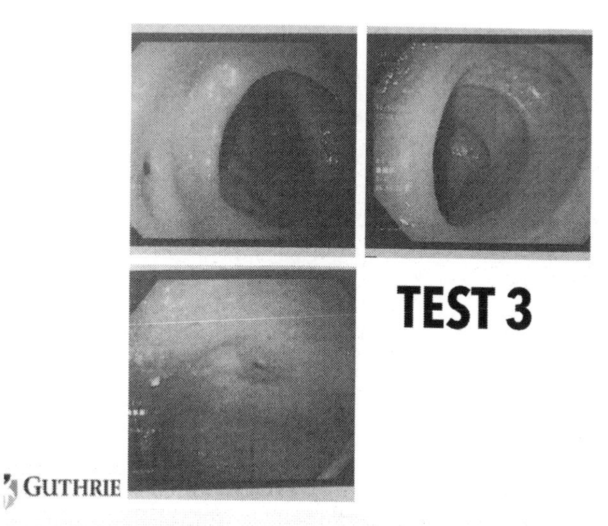

RPH ENDOSCOPY CENTER

RHONDA J SPENCER

RE: Spencer, Rhonda

DOB

Dear Ms. Spencer :

I am writing this letter concerning the recent Flexiable sigmoidoscopy that was performed at the Guthrie Clinic in Sayre,PA on October 17,2016. As you may recall, we did obtain biopsies during the examination.

The biopsies showed no dysplasia. **TEST 3**

I hope this correspondence finds you well. If you have any questions regarding this information, or if any problems arise, please do not hesitate to call

Sincerely,

Preetika Sinh, MD

Elizabeth A Hickey, RN 10/19/1612:56

CC: Daugherty, Shannon

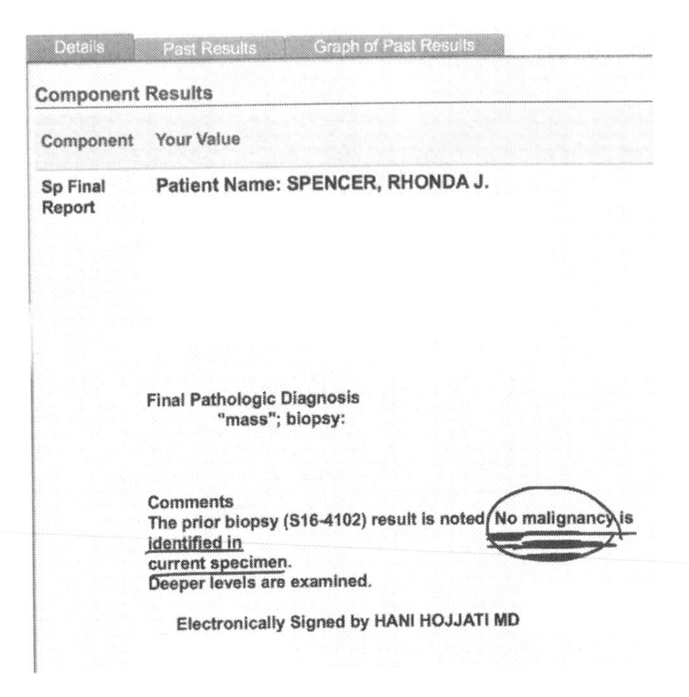
Details | Past Results | Graph of Past Results

Component Results

Component	Your Value
Sp Final Report	Patient Name: SPENCER, RHONDA J.

Final Pathologic Diagnosis
"mass"; biopsy:

Comments
The prior biopsy (S16-4102) result is noted. No malignancy is identified in current specimen.
Deeper levels are examined.

Electronically Signed by HANI HOJJATI MD

I was healed of cancer. It was gone from my body.

But wait! The miracle was only the beginning of my "fight the good fight of faith."

The miracle is just what our compassionate loving God does. It was after the miracle that I had the most struggle with people's spoken words, doctors, and my own gut theologies.

NO FEAR

Fear is often the first, and one of the greatest battles that come when we are facing a mountain in our lives. Fear tells us that we will never make it through, that we will die and not live. However, as children of God, we are led by the Spirit of God.

We are not led by lies, we are not led by our own minds, we are not led by people's words, and we are **not led by fear**.

2 Timothy 1:7 "For God hath not given us the <u>spirit of fear</u>; but of power, and of love, and of a sound mind" KJV

Let's identify and expose fear:

Fear is not from God.

As we saw in the above scripture, God has not given us the spirit of fear. Fear is from the devil and is a spirit that works in our hearts and minds. We are to give him and his tactic of fear absolutely no place in our lives.

James 4:7 "Submit yourselves therefore to God. Resist the devil, and he will flee from you." KJV

2 Corinthians 3:17 "Now the Lord is the Spirit, and where the Spirit of the Lord is, there is liberty." NASB

The Spirit of the Lord is liberty, not fear!

Do not do anything from a place of fear.

Fear is the spirit of the enemy of our soul. We know that it is not from God, yet so many times we act and react out of fear, and ultimately find ourselves being led by the fear.

Psalms 46:1-2 "God is our refuge and strength, always ready to help in times of trouble. So we will not fear when earthquakes come and the mountains crumble into the sea."NLT

Matthew 14:27-31 "But Jesus spoke to them at once. 'Don't be afraid,' he said. 'Take courage. I am here!' Then Peter called to him, 'Lord, if it's really you, tell me to come to you, walking on the water.' 'Yes, come,' Jesus said. So Peter went over the side of the boat and walked on the water toward Jesus. But when he saw the strong wind and the waves, he was terrified and began to sink. 'Save me, Lord!' he shouted. Jesus immediately reached out and grabbed him. 'You have so little faith,' Jesus said. 'Why did you doubt me?'"NLT

It is easy to begin to fear when the storm and winds come...in our family...in our health...in our work places...in our finances...when people start to prattle and say all manner of things about you. It may feel like the world is crumbling and falling apart. But when we respond out of fear, we will begin to sink just like Peter did. The devil would love to see us drown.

Remember, fear and faith are complete opposites.

It is impossible to look in opposite directions at the same time.

You can either focus on fear or on faith. In fact, fear actually cancels faith right out. Even if that lousy voice of fear seems to be the loudest voice in our head, we cannot afford to sacrifice our faith to it, to give it a greater place than our faith.

1 John 4:18 "Such love has no fear, because perfect love expels all fear. If we are afraid, it is for fear of punishment, and this shows that we have not fully experienced his perfect love."NLT

Psalms 37:39 "The lord rescues the godly; he is their fortress in times of trouble." NLT

Lamentations 3:21-23 "Yet I still dare to hope when I remember this: The faithful love of the lord never ends! His compassions never cease. Great is his faithfulness; his mercies begin afresh each morning." NLT

Philippians 4:6-7 "Don't worry about anything; instead, pray about everything. Tell God what you need, and thank him for all he has done. Then you will experience God's peace, which exceeds anything we can understand. His peace will guard your hearts and minds as you live in Christ Jesus." NLT

Ephesians 1:11 "Furthermore, because we are united with Christ, we have received an inheritance from God, for he chose us in advance, and he makes everything work out according to his plan." NLT

2 Samuel 2:2 "No one is holy like the Lord! There is no one besides you; there is no Rock like our God." NLT

Living led by the Spirit of God is to live fearless.

Hebrews 13:5-6 "**I will never** [under any circumstances] **desert you** [nor give you up nor leave you without support, nor will I in any degree leave you helpless], **nor will I forsake you** or **let you down** or **relax my hold on you** [assuredly not]!" So we take comfort and are encouraged and confidently say, "**The Lord is my helper** [in time of need], **I will not be afraid.**" AMP

Isaiah 43:1-2, 5 "The one who formed you says, 'Do not be afraid, for I have ransomed you. I have called you by name; you are mine. When you go through deep waters, I will be with you. When you go through rivers of difficulty, you will not drown. When you walk through the fire of oppression, you will not be burned up; the flames will not consume you. Do not be afraid, for I am with you.'" NLT

When fear comes in and takes your breath away, remember that it does not come from God. Do NOT respond out of that fear.

Fear comes from the lying devil. All he does is lie. Just because the devil is talking to you does not mean that you have to respond to him.

Whenever you hear fear talking in your ear, you can automatically know that it is a lie, and that the exact opposite is true. When Satan gets us to think wrong, he achieves his desire for us to forfeit our security in Jesus. Fear will cause us to forsake our belief in the power of God.

When our confidence is in Jesus and His Word, we will be fearless. Besides, since we call ourselves "believers," we ought to actually **believe**. Believe God over the lies of fear. **God cannot lie**.

The Word of God should be the basis of our trust. We should love the Word and value it so much that we automatically hold it up above any fear that tries to come in.

Is it not more rational as a Christian, as a believer in God, for us to trust God and NOT FEARS?

Whenever we become affected by any voice more than we are affected by the voice of God (His Word), we are not acting as believers. It becomes easy to then base our belief system on our past circumstances, situations, and things that happened, rather than on the Word of God, thus swinging the door wide open for fear, inviting it in.

Every time we answer with "yeah but" we are excusing the power of God right out of our situation and allowing fear to rule and reign in our hearts and minds.

Every "yeah but" takes us away from being a believer and trusting in the word of God. No wonder we have been unable to see God move. Every time our mind thinks: "yeah but," we need to quickly exchange that with, "It is written!" After that, we need to lift up our praise and thanksgiving right in the face of fear.

Jesus already made an open show of the defeated enemy.

(Colossians 2:15)

Why would we then allow, even for a second, the voice of fear to torment us? If we resist the devil, **he must flee**.

To resist something means something has to be coming at you that needs to be resisted. So when fear comes at you, do not be surprised by it, but do resist it! Cancel its assignment, and its intended purpose, and replace it with the Word of God.

Isaiah 55:11 "It is the same with My Word. I send it out, and it always produces fruit. It will accomplish all I want it to, and it will prosper everywhere I send it."NLT

Just because a package is delivered to your doorstep does not mean you have to receive it. I remember when we had a delivery of a very nice handcrafted, very expensive, wooden canoe. We had not ordered it or paid for it, so we refused to keep it. Although it was delivered to us, we would never want to get stuck paying the price for something that we did not order nor did we want. Do not receive the package the enemy is delivering, because you do not want to get stuck paying for it. Fear is from the enemy of your soul. It is never from God.

Mark 5:36 "Do not be afraid, only believe."NKJV

Psalm 3:6 "I will not be afraid of ten thousands of people who have set themselves against me round about." NKJV

Psalm 27:3 "Though a host encamp against me, My heart will not fear; Though war arise against me, In spite of this I shall be confident." NASB

Psalm 46:2 "Therefore we will not fear, though the earth should change And though the mountains slip into the heart of the sea."NASB

Psalm 91:5 "You will not be afraid of the terror by night, or of the arrow that flies by day."NASB

Proverbs 3:24 "When you lie down, you will not be afraid; when you lie down, your sleep will be sweet."NASB

Isaiah 12:2 "Behold, God is my salvation, I will trust and not be afraid; For the LORD GOD is my strength and song, and He has become my salvation."NASB

Let's pray together right now: Father, in the name of Jesus I bind up the spirit of fear from operating in my life. I know fear does not come from You, so I reject its package. I choose to not allow any fear in, but I choose to walk in faith only. Thank You that You have given me the power to overcome anything and everything that I am facing today. You are the same yesterday, today, and forever and You still do miracles. I know that You will do a miracle for me. In Jesus name I pray, amen.

Because we haven't
seen it happen
We don't believe it will happen
and because we don't
believe it will happen
we will never see it happen.

#Cycleofunbelief
#Breakthecycle
Believe
with God
nothing
is impossible.

Be encouraged by this awesome testimony of God's miracle-working power today, that I received recently from a member of our congregation:

"One morning I woke up feeling very sick, but I did not take much notice and figured it would pass. As the day progressed, I felt worse and worse. I ended up hospitalized with a fever of 106, low blood pressure and a very high heart rate. After a spinal tap and blood work, I was sent home without any answers whatsoever. In the following weeks, things got rapidly worse. I had severe neck pain and back pain, I could not stand up without feeling dizzy, and I felt extremely fatigued.
During these weeks, I was tested for MS, meningitis, mono, lyme disease, and tick-born illnesses. I was sent to several different specialists and with every test that came back negative, I began to mentally deflate. I slowly convinced myself I would not be able to watch my children grow up. The fears of what could be began taking over my mind.
After one straight month of living this way, I told my husband that I needed to get to church. I had been praying faithfully, but I had been so sick I thought I could not make it to church.
We made it to church, and I went right to the altar. I could not stand at the altar because the pain was so bad, so I asked for someone's front seat. As I sat there during worship, I began

crying and praying. Pastor Rhonda Spencer came over to me, and she asked me if I needed prayer. First, she prayed for my doubts and fears to go away. For me, this was unbelievable, because I had not told anyone my fears that were overtaking me. Next, she prayed for me physically. I cannot explain the overwhelming sense of calm that came over me as I cried and received her prayers. I truly felt, for the first time, that I was surrendering my sickness at the cross.

I went home from church that day and told my husband ALL of the pain was gone. I realized, at that moment, I was not afraid anymore either.

I played outside with my children and even baked my husband an apple pie that day. Although I was healed, I still went to bed afraid that I would wake up, and it would all be back. But it was not! I woke up the next day and I was 100% okay. I let all doubts go, and I found my mind was finally doubt and worry free about my future.

Doctors were baffled and continued to run tests. They also continued sending me to specialists testing for different things, but I stand firm that I am healed! It has been 6 months since then and I have been 100% symptom free!"

~ Jody Smith

DON'T ACCEPT IT, FOR ANY REASON

Do not give up & do not GIVE IN!

There is NO reason for sickness to be on you. Christ paid the FULL price on the cross.

2 Corinthians 1:20 "For all of God's promises have been fulfilled in Christ with a resounding "Yes!" and through Christ, our "Amen" (which means "Yes") ascends to God for his glory."NLT

Nothing. NO THING has any effect on the oath and promise of God, other than our own free will.

Hebrews 6:17-18 "God also bound himself with an oath, so that those who received the promise could be perfectly sure that He would never change His mind. So God has given both His promise and His oath. These two things are unchangeable because it is impossible for God to lie. Therefore, we who have fled to Him for refuge can have great confidence as we hold to the hope that lies before us."NLT

God will never tempt, test, or punish us with that for which He paid the ultimate and immeasurable price to conquer for us on the cross. Our sins & sicknesses were paid for by the precious blood of Jesus. It was the perfect sacrifice. It was God's great love for us, a gift.

As long as I come up with reasons why I am sick, or work from "gut theologies," I am not actually standing in faith.

Mark 7:13 "...so you nullify the [authority of the] word of God [acting as if it did not apply] because of your tradition which you have handed down [through the elders]. And you do many things such as that." AMP

A "gut theology" is what we think about the Word of God deep in our subconscious, and how we personally interpret it based on our own thoughts and experiences. Gut theologies could include thoughts like; "Unforgiveness has made me sick." "I must have done something wrong, and that is why I am not getting healed," etc.

When God healed me, one of the craziest statements I began to hear was; "You were healed because you are a pastor's wife." As if to say that that made me something special and placed me at the very front of the healing line. But, boy, no one who said that was there when I had to sit through numerous doctor appointments and stare death right in the face. No one was around when, after standing, I had to *stand therefore* even when it felt like I was on sinking sand. No one was there when I had to decide to push past what I felt and still fight the good fight of faith. I wish it was that easy to be healed, just because I was "someone special."

God desires to heal everyone. He is no respecter of persons

Hallelujah! Yet many of us allow our gut theologies and unbiblical thoughts to give us an excuse to accept sickness and disease in our bodies.

Stop finding reasons to accept it. Fight to reject that package and return it right back to the sender!

Another excuse we often use is finances. We attempt to base the chances of our healing on what is financially available. As if to believe that the person next to us was healed, and we were not, because they have a better financial status and, thus, better access to the best medical professionals. Yet again, here we are accepting a natural reason when, in the supernatural realm, none of that matters. We have Christ our Healer who, based on His Word, desires to heal anyone and everyone. As if excuses are not enough, we then move on to finding a "good reason" to accept the sickness or disease, and, then, revive it rather than fight and reject it.

Early on in my diagnosis, my husband and I were speaking with a man of God who's response to the report was; "This is an attack of the enemy because of all the good things you are doing." While this statement was very true, one of the things that happened quickly in my mind was that I actually accepted the attack, because I had a "good reason" to. But thank God, as quickly as I accepted it, I rejected it.

Do not fall for any reasons why this sickness is on you. Only remain in the mode that rejects and fights it.

I wish that I knew then what I know now; we had a very dear beloved pastor who was very close to our family, who had been diagnosed with cancer. I remember him coming to us and revealing the reason he believed he was suffering. He had deep bitterness in his heart towards his wife, of which he could not let go. Instead of making the decision to forgive, he accepted it as his lot in life.

The same God that heals also forgives us of all of our sins. Salvation is a package deal.

Knowing what I know now, I would have encouraged him and told him that he could be forgiven of bitterness and healed of the sickness. I would have responded that we are not to accept sickness for ANY reason.

Unbelief or bad religion in our brains has caused us to scan and scan and scan, trying desperately to find a reason for what we do not understand. The problem? **Any reason is acceptance.**

1 Corinthians 6:19-20 "Or do you not know that your body is the temple of the Holy Spirit who is in you, whom you have from God, and you are not your own? For you were bought at a price; therefore glorify God in your body and in your spirit, which are God's."NKJV

Not one of us would accept someone trespassing on our property, especially not on a regular basis. Yet we allow sickness to trespass where it does not belong. Our body is the property of the Spirit of God;

paid for by **the death of His Son on the cross!**

The enemy has not only trespassed on you, he has trespassed on

***the precious blood of Jesus*.**

DEVIL, FEAR THIS!!! You have trespassed on the precious blood of JESUS!

My body IS
the property of
the Spirit of God
paid for by the price
of His son's life on a cross!
The enemy has not only
trespassed on my body
he has trespassed on
THE PRECIOUS
SHED BLOOD OF JESUS!!!
...devil you FEAR THIS!!!

There is no "acceptable" reason for sickness to remain on us as children of God.

As His children and heirs to all of His promises, the same God who heals us and forgives us of our sin is the same God who accepts us into His family. The best packages are never left out on your doorstep - accept it today.

Proverbs 6:2 "You are snared by the words of your mouth; You are taken by the words of your mouth." NKJV

Philippians 4:8 "Finally, brethren, whatsoever things are true [*as the Word is*], whatsoever things are honest, whatsoever things are just, whatsoever things are pure, whatsoever things are lovely, whatsoever things are of good report; if there be any virtue, and if there be any praise, think on these things." ASV

Proverbs 23:7a
"For as he thinketh in his heart, so is he." KJV

Isaiah 30:12-19 "This is the reply of the Holy One of Israel: 'Because **you despise what I tell you and trust instead in oppression and lies**, calamity will come upon you suddenly—like a bulging wall that bursts and falls.

In an instant it will collapse and come crashing down.
You will be smashed like a piece of pottery – shattered so completely that there won't be a piece big enough to carry coals from a fireplace or a little water from the well.'
This is what the Sovereign Lord, the Holy One of Israel, says:
'Only in returning to me and resting in me will you be saved.
In quietness and confidence is your strength.
But you would have none of it.'
You said, 'No, we will get our help from Egypt.
They will give us swift horses for riding into battle.
But the only swiftness you are going to see is the swiftness of your enemies chasing you!
One of them will chase a thousand of you.
Five of them will make all of you flee.
You will be left like a lonely flagpole on a hill or a tattered banner on a distant mountaintop.'
So the Lord must wait for you to come to him so he can show you his love and compassion.
For the Lord is a faithful God.
Blessed are those who wait for his help.
O people of Zion, who live in Jerusalem, you will weep no more.
He will be gracious if you ask for help.
He will surely respond to the sound of your cries." NLT

Hebrews 4:2 "For this good news—that God has prepared this rest—has been announced to us just as it was to them. But **it did them no good because they didn't share the faith of those who listened to God**."NLT

No matter how long you have been believing, keep standing on faith!!!!! My daughter-in-law, Mindy wears pretty significant glasses and has actively been believing God to heal her eyes for 5 years (it was easy for her to accept it and just wear glasses). At one point she even determined to just take her glasses off...still no healing. SHE DIDN'T GIVE UP OR QUIT BELIEVING THOUGH!!! Recently she asked to have her eyes prayed for AGAIN. SHE IS HEALED!!!!!! She saw all new refractions of light and can read the tiny time of day on her husbands phone next to her!!!!! She can read the road sign info now and is seeing, with her own eyes, new things she was unable to see before!!!
DON'T ACCEPT SICKNESS OR DISEASE FOR ANY REASON. Don't give up and don't quit believing. GOD WILL HEAL YOU TOO, there's no reason why He wants you to keep sickness, pain or disease (nope NONE).

MY OUTLOOK

It's all in how we view God.

I am sure you have had uncomfortable and unpleasant circumstances, at one time or another, that were out of your control. We all have. Maybe you are even facing one right now, as you flip through the pages of this book. The Bible warns us that in this fallen world, we will have troubles. So we have to know that difficult and unpleasant circumstances (usually completely out of our control) will happen.

The issue, then, is not whether they will happen, but how we respond to them when they do. Our outlook is where we have all the power; controlling our peace, controlling our joy, controlling our love, which will ultimately control how we respond and move on.

Although we do not enjoy these circumstances (far from it), James 1 exhorts us to rejoice when trials come our way. Why? Because, how we choose to handle the circumstances will put us in control of how we will feel during the day. The way we look at a trial changes our day. It changes how we feel in the right now. The power is solely in our hands.

You are not powerless.

When we choose to live every new day with hope and faith as our primary driving forces, we remain in absolute peace, because we know we are positioned perfectly in God's ever-secure hands.

Romans 8:28 "And we know that God causes everything to work together for the good of those who love God and are called according to his purpose for them."NLT

One of my favorite quotes goes perfectly with what we have been talking about, **"I can complain because rosebushes have thorns or I can rejoice because thorn bushes have roses."** It is all about how you look at it.

After realizing just how important my outlook on a circumstance is, I was able to receive a greater understanding of Philippians 4, where Paul encourages us to be anxious for nothing. Honestly, what does anxiety do for us, except steal our joy, our peace, and our security?

Nehemiah 8:10 "Don't be dejected and sad, for the joy of the Lord is your strength!"NLT

Not one good thing ever comes from negative thinking. However, when we line up our thinking with the Word of God, something good always comes out of that!

The way you think is directly connected with the way you feel. So, if you want to change the way you feel, go directly to the root and correct the way you are thinking. How? By "washing our minds with the Word of God" as we see in Ephesians 5:26.

Find the roses on those thorn bushes of life and consciously decide to dwell on those good things. Watch just how quickly your day will change in the midst of unpleasant circumstances.

Deuteronomy 30:19 "Today I have given you the choice between life and death, between blessings and curses. Now I call on heaven and earth to witness the choice you make. Oh, that you would choose life, so that you and your descendants might live!"NLT

Every day can be a good day!

Look at the rose bush...blessing and cursing set before you. Whatever you focus on will take over your vision: Thorns or Roses. Cut off some stems of those rose bushes and put them on display in a vase on the table. There are thorns and roses still, but choose to celebrate beauty.

MY THOUGHTS & VAIN IMAGINATIONS: THE REAL BATTLE

The devil is a lot like the media, he only reports one-sided and terrible news. Why? Because good news, unfortunately, never sells like bad news does. With that in mind, I want you to remember, right now, that the devil is a liar. Not only that, but he is the *father* of lies. His reporting is bad news and far from the truth. The opposite of what he says is actually what is true.

As Christians living life in this world governed by the powers of darkness, it is very easy to forget who God really is, and who we are in Him. He desires to dwell within us. Our time with Him should not be a one time contact, but, instead a consistent union.

Romans 8:11 "And if the Spirit of him who raised Jesus from the dead is living in you, he who raised Christ from the dead will also give life to your mortal bodies because of his Spirit who lives in you" NIV

John 15:5, 7-9, 11 "I am the Vine; you are the branches. The one who remains in Me and I in him bears much fruit, for [otherwise] apart from Me [that is, cut off from vital union with Me] you can do nothing. If you remain in Me and My words remain in you [that is, if we are vitally united and My message lives in your heart], ask whatever you wish and it will be done for you. My Father is glorified and honored by this, when you bear much fruit, and prove yourselves to be My [true] disciples. I have loved you just as the Father has loved Me; remain in My love [and do not doubt My love for you]. I have told you these things so that My joy and delight may be in you, and that your joy may be made full and complete and overflowing." AMP

Literally, as the life source of the branches is the vine, so our life source and all its power is God Himself. When we live so much by the circumstances that come and go, like them, we are tossed to and fro, forgetting that

our connection to the Vine actually makes us stable and secure.

The power and presence of the Almighty God is ours to have, as long as we stay united with Him.

We need to walk by faith and not by sight.

Our faith remains only hypothetical until we have to use it.

Revelation 3 talks about the danger of being found lukewarm by the Lord, and how it displeases Him. In the Amplified Bible, it explains lukewarm to be "spiritually useless". When we are in a battle, there is no time or place to be "spiritually useless."

Revelation 3:15-16 "I know your deeds, that you are neither cold (invigorating, refreshing) nor hot (healing, therapeutic); I wish that you were cold or hot. ~'So because you are lukewarm (spiritually useless), and neither hot nor cold, I will vomit you out of My mouth [rejecting you with disgust]." AMP

If we are in battle (and life *is* a battle) and our faith is dormant, we are spiritually useless. No wonder we are discouraged, tired, sick and weary!

We need to believe who God is and that He is a rewarder of those who diligently seek Him according to Hebrews 11.

When we have become fully convinced of who God is and believe what His Word declares, we have officially moved into the space of mountain-moving faith.

Our identity as a branch connected to THE VINE, will change the battle. We need to walk in it and keep standing on it until we are convinced of it. How? By taking any other thought that is contrary captive, and bringing it into obedience before God. God's truth is our sure foundation - our anchor and very life source.

I mentioned this scripture earlier;
Jonah 2:7-9 "When my soul fainted within me, I remembered Jehovah; And my prayer came in unto Thee, into Thy holy temple. They that regard lying vanities forsake their own mercy. But I will sacrifice unto Thee with the voice of thanksgiving; I will pay that which I have vowed. Salvation (*sozo* - "complete wholeness") is of Jehovah." ASV

They that regard lying vanities forsake their own mercy.

We must reject any "lying vanities" that come to steal our joy, kill our hope and destroy our lives. Any word spoken, report given, or diagnosis that is contrary to what God's Word says, we must forsake. God's Word is our truth, God's Word is MY truth!

This Truth makes us free; free from fear, doubt, depression, discouragement, sickness, disease, pain, sin, and the list goes on.

Just like in the natural it would be impossible for soldiers to win a war in a sloppy and uninterested state, so it is impossible to win a battle in a lukewarm and spiritually useless state. This explains why many Christians are in the battle, but are not coming out victorious. The good news? A simple choice can flip our situation in an instant. Let's make the decision together to reconnect to the Vine that gives us life.

The same power that flowed out of Jesus into the woman who touched His garment and was made immediately whole is the same power that is IN US! This is something to get excited about!

Almost a year ago, my husband and I were sitting together eating breakfast with Bishop Rick Thomas, senior pastor of Abundant Life Church in Margate, Florida. The topic of confession and believing came up and, almost immediately, I traded the crossword puzzle, that I had intently been working on, for a notepad to write down every piece of wisdom the man of God began to speak. Allow me to share them with you right now:

The Bible says the following in Mark 11:22-23, "Have faith in God. Whoever says (your confession) to this mountain and does not doubt in his heart, but believes, he will have whatever he says." The Bible also talks in Matthew 21 about receiving what we ask for as well as in James 1.

Confession and believing are tricky subjects in the Church today, because many of us have been condemned for making dramatic statements. I guarantee we have all had a moment of flippantly saying something just to receive the response of; "Well, you can have what you say."

The only time it's a bad confession is when you believe the negative you are speaking.

Maybe you have said something along the lines of, "It's so hot out I'm gonna die." You do not really believe that you are going to die do you? Exactly, it is then not the feared "bad confession."

Unfortunately, we have made doctrine and theology out of what we merely say (most times in the heat of the moment). It does not actually, really matter what someone says. What matters is the faith behind it. We do indeed need to be cautious that our faith does not back up silly statements, especially not more than the Word of God. Our confession is nothing without believing.

What I don't believe doesn't matter.

If it was really true that whatever we said would happen, all we would have to do would be speak the Word of God and it would happen. How awesome!

We do need to heed ourselves to the fact that just because we are able to quote Scripture does not necessarily mean that what we are quoting is real to us as heart knowledge. The devil can, and does, quote Scripture too. Do you remember in Matthew 45 when Jesus was in the wilderness? The devil even used the term, "It is written."

Going through the motions is not a fruitful and powerful way to live. Faith is not a mathematical formula that works on paper - it comes from the heart. What we truly believe is what we will receive. Disappointment occurs when we fail to apply our faith, yet expect great miracles.

"But I'm quoting the Word of God!"
"I'm declaring what the word of God says."
"Why am I not seeing it happen?"
Confess and believe. Hebrews 11:6 lets us know that it is impossible to please God without faith.

It honestly does not matter what you say, if you don't believe it.

Our words can be empty and hollow all by themselves. And that is sometimes where the battle lies: we hear the Word, we can speak and declare the Word, but we struggle with *believing* that it is for us, for now or today.

Luke 6:45 "Out of the abundance of the heart the mouth speaks." NKJV

Hebrews 4:2 "For indeed we have had good news preached to us, just as they also; but **the word they heard did not profit them**, **because it was not united by faith in those who heard.**" NASB

I love the story in Numbers 13 and 14 about the twelve spies; ten of them spoke what they believed out of fear. The giants of the land did not defeat them, they defeated themselves with what they spoke and believed in their heart. Only two of the spies came back with reports of faith: even though the giants in the land were very real, they knew that God would be with them and help them to take the land. Those two men were the only two from their entire generation that were able to enter into the promised land! **The giants that the others feared were the same giants that the two spies believed they could defeat, and therefore they did.**

It is all reliant on what you believe and speak.

Here's a practical scenario: a man heard, like many of us have, that when you get older your memory is the first thing to go (be careful of actually believing that). When the man heard that the mind is the first thing to go, he began to speak it, and then believed it. What do you think happened next? Well, soon he could not remember things and found himself getting more and more frustrated. Thankfully, he heard the truth that we, as children of God, have the mind of Christ (1 Corinthians 2:16). So he began to change what he spoke and believed. Soon enough everything began to change and his memory was restored.

Believing and speaking will work in both ways, in the positive and in the negative.

We can walk in healing, prosperity, peace, and blessing if we believe it in our heart and confess it with our mouth. Or we can struggle, not receive anything from God, and remain sick and defeated, if that is what we believe and confess with our mouth.

Mark 11:22-23 "Have faith in God, whoever SAYS to this mountain AND does not doubt in his heart but BELIEVES he will have whatever he says" NASB *emphasis mine*

Here is another awesome testimony that I received recently from my daughter-in-law:

"Around Thanksgiving time, I began to notice a subtle throbbing in the right side of my face and jaw. I really did not think too much about it and shrugged it off as a what I thought must have been a sinus infection. I began to realize that there was more going on when the pain only grew worse and worse over the next couple of days, to the point where I was not able to eat, sleep or even speak much. I was in agony. Eventually, my husband put his foot down. I remember driving to the ER at 2am and thinking, "Is this really happening to me?"

After being hooked up to an IV for fluids and having a thorough examination followed by a plethora of health questions, the nurse left the room to discuss the symptoms with her superior. "Trigeminal Neuralgia, a nerve disorder in the facial region" was the starting statement pouring out of the doctor's mouth as he rushed back into the room. As if that diagnosis was not enough, he went on to tell me that this would be a recurrent agony in my life, and that facial surgery was most likely necessary. He also told me that the likelihood of my face drooping was common. He also, very apologetically, let me know that because the issue was with the nerves, pain medication would not effectively relieve any pain.

Because there was nothing more that they could do, I was sent home.

For as long as I live, I will never forget the tangible time between God and me as I lay on the floor of the shower (I was just too weak to stand) and began to talk with Him. I reminded Him that I was His child and that healing was my portion. I reminded Him that I served Him with my whole heart, and I preached His Word faithfully. I got to the point of being so completely desperate in His presence that I told Him that, if He did not heal me, I would no longer serve Him. Why, you may be wondering? Because that would make Him a liar, and I do not serve a liar.

I tell you what, I got out of the shower a whole different woman. Still in pain, I told my husband to go downstairs and to get the olive oil, he needed to anoint my face. Faith flooded my body like I have never experienced it before. After he anointed and prayed over my body, I got myself dressed and requested to be taken to church. I wanted my oversight to pray for my body too.
Immediately, as my pastor laid his hands on my face, I felt relief - it was not complete, but it was relief still. My faith did not waiver. Actually, as they went into our sanctuary for service, I fell asleep soundly on the church office couch, the first time in three days.

I was scheduled to fly to South Africa the very next day with my mother-in-law (Pastor Rhonda), as she was the guest speaker of a women's conference at my home church there. Ministry was waiting, sickness was not an option. Church wrapped up, and I woke up to my husband getting ready to take me home to pack my bags for my upcoming trip. I will be honest - in the natural, I saw no way of getting on a sixteen hour flight, or going anywhere in general. Again, that is when my faith had to take the front seat. I went to bed praising God and thanking Him for my healing. At 3am, when my alarm went off, I dragged my body to the shower, where I was washing my hair like I did on any day, I stood dead still and yelled out; "Chad, I have no pain!" Every inch of pain had completely left my body! Yes, my natural body was tired. Yes, my facial region was tight, but I was healed. God gave me a 24 hour miracle!

I arrived in South Africa just ecstatic about God's goodness and faithfulness. We had an incredible time, and women were impacted! But I want to be honest with you - yes, I was healed, but *there were still symptoms*. I do not think we should be surprised about this, the enemy is MAD. But we need to be prepared, and many of us are not. Many begin to question whether or not healing even really took place. Doubt arises and we give up. I knew that only God could have done in my body what He did. So for every symptom that raised its head, I shot it back down with the rich and true Word of God.

I stand here today, busier than ever with ministry, healthy in my body, and firmly rooted in my God and His promises. With a smile that does not sag or droop in any way! Hallelujah!"

~ *Jade Spencer*

FINDING FAITH?

It is always God's will to heal you.

When I was faced with the mountain of cancer, I needed to draw from the well of faith inside of me. I had genuinely considered myself a person of extreme faith and so I did not think twice as I excitedly lowered the bucket down into my heart to draw from my personal well of faith. When I pulled the bucket back up expecting to find faith, I was surprised at what I found: thoughts and reasons, my "gut theologies" and unspoken fears. So many of them in there, that I actually had to sort through them in the hope of finding faith somewhere, anywhere.

"Is there sin in my life?"
"Maybe I am not one of the "special ones?"
"How could this even happen to me?"
"Why is this happening to me?"
"Do I have unforgiveness in my heart?"
"Sins of the fathers?"
"Is there a curse on my life?"
"Did I speak words to create this?"
"Is this from God, for His glory?"
"I am going to die."

I found that the key to finding faith is to look deep on the inside and honestly sort through any wrong thoughts or "gut theologies" that I may have picked up along the way due to things I had seen or experienced. These things were hidden so deep down inside of me - in my subconscious - that I had to really dig them out in order to discover believing for myself. I discovered that not believing for ourselves is really no belief at all.

Everything that was against the truth of God had to be thrown away.

I had to replace every thought wedged deeply in my subconscious mind with the freeing truth of God's Word. Through saturation, the Word became my confidence. But what a battle! When the Word of God summons us to "fight the good fight of faith," it is not a hypothetical fight with unrealistic expectations. It is as real as it gets.

I had to intentionally fight off all wrong thoughts and ideas: habitual responses and cliche answers not found in the Word of God. There was no alternative in which I would find my faith. It was the Word and the Word alone that I found faith in.

As my husband had the Bible playing throughout our home 24/7, it began to outweigh every other negative thought, declaration, or diagnosis. My faith got stronger and stronger, and so did my confidence. Romans 10:17 proves this; "So faith comes from hearing, that is, hearing the Good News about Christ."NLT

So, if you or anyone you know needs to kick out fear and doubt and replace it with faith, ***hear the Word of God***. Whether you read it or listen to it: submerse yourself in nothing but the Word of God.

It was only at the end of the sorting process, that I truly found pure faith. True, genuine faith, founded on the fact that our God *cannot* lie. As surely as gravity is in effect, and as surely as the sun will rise – my God cannot lie.

What NOT to say to or about someone who is clinging to life:

Never in a million years, especially with years of ministry behind me, did I ever think that facing a personal mountain, as a Christian in the church, would be as difficult as I found it to be. In my mind, I thought the House of God would be the best place to be when facing something. And it should be, but the problem is that in any church there are people, like you and me, who have well-meaning hearts with their own "gut theologies" and standard ways of responding. Hence the personal mountain not being the easiest thing to move in that moment. I am not saying this because I believe it is not good to be in the church. The only place I would want to be facing a personal mountain is in the church. I am saying this so you'll gain understanding and not get upset with the well-meaning people. I am also saying it so you will recognize it in yourself.

Please know that I am talking from the place of personal experience that was inside me. God revealed this ugliness and lack of faith *in me*. I am so thankful! Not only did it change the way I prayed and believed for others, but it was the key to unlocking the genuine faith needed for a miracle in me.

John 10:10 "The thief does not come except to steal, and to kill, and to destroy. I have come that they may have life, and that they may have *it* more abundantly." NKJV

We, as the Church, need to wake up and pay careful attention to the severity of this scripture. According to God's written Word, it is the ***devil*** who comes to steal, to kill, and to destroy. As God's precious children and priceless possessions, we want nothing to do with what the enemy of life is doing. We must only be part of *life*, and *life in abundance*.

So, because of this experience and how my earnest expectation dimmed with disappointment when coming into contact with harsh reality, I want to share with you what I felt and learned. I believe that with a little training, we can better meet others in their need and help each of us find faith for ourselves.

Proverbs 18:21 says; "Death and life are in the power of the tongue." Wow, the tongue. We hold such great power in such a small portion of our body. **What we say to and believe about others can either destroy or bring healing.** This is so exciting, yet very scary at the same time. I never want to use the power that was given to me to heal and bring life, to destroy and bring death. I want it to heal and bring life.

This seemingly simple revelation of God's great Word will totally transform how you speak, pray, and believe. Ask yourself: How am I wielding my power? Now is a great time for us to conduct a real, honest life-check. Am I judging and condemning? Am I part of the problem instead of the solution?

When someone is fighting for their life, their feelings may differ depending on the intensity of the circumstance. There may be days of, "I am going to be okay, thank You Jesus!" and, then, there may be the very real days of, "I would rather die than fight this." I know I had fleeting moments of these lies in my mind.

Friend, I know that it is not easy when the thoughts that overcome your mind are the complete opposite of what you are declaring. I know what it is like to not understand and to feel the weight of condemnation on your shoulders. Take heart because, although we do not always understand why the facts have not yet changed, it DOES NOT MEAN that there is something wrong with your faith, that you have sin in your life, or that God is a liar.

So fight every thought that raises itself up against God's truth and just trust.

God cannot lie, He will uphold you, and you will get through!

What people need to hear in those moments of uncertainty is that you understand this may be the hardest thing they have ever gone through. That you realize it is scary, and that things seem unsure. That even though they feel alone, they are not, and that God is a miracle-working God who is true to what His Word promises. God is no respecter of persons. He is the same miracle worker today that He was yesterday and will be forever. Let them know that you will stand in agreement with them to see a miracle occur and will be faithful to pray with and for them, upholding them in the fight.

Our judgements, reasons why, and excuses will not produce the faith that is needed to move mountains. Because of the devil's awful tactics, it is probable they are already aware that they need to check their heart for unforgiveness, or any other sin. However, if you feel led to share with them on the power of forgiveness, do so with love and care.

The disease: that is nothing for God. The fight, however, is in our mind, with the devil, and with well-meaning people.

Let us put ourselves in the shoes of someone who is weak and trying hard to cling to life. What would you want to hear in that moment? You certainly would not want someone "standing in agreement" with you who has judgmental thoughts and reasons as to why you are dealing with what you have going on. You would want a faith injection! *Be* that faith injection for someone else. When they pull up the bucket from the well on the inside, let there be reminders of your words based on

Scripture, and your unwavering prayers. We must believe that God will heal everyone, including us. We must put all of our petty judgements aside and allow faith to take over.

We cannot have reasons, excuses, judgement or condemnation, and have faith at the same time.

Compassion like this is the key to ministering miracles. This is exactly how and why Jesus healed every person of every disease. He did not have pre-conceived judgements, reasons, or excuses about why people were sick. He just knew that He would forgive them of their sins and heal them of their diseases. His great and sincere compassion healed both the sinner and the saint. He even delivered those that were full of the devil.

As onlookers, we must believe that our God is a miracle worker, and that He healed everyone who came to Him. There were no special circumstances and nothing too big that would exempt anyone from God's miracle power, not even sin. Our God performed miracles and then said, "Go and sin no more." He will forgive all sins and heal all diseases.

I recently heard a story of a pastor's wife who was diagnosed with cancer. Some of the members of the congregation got judgement and condemnation in their minds about it and left the church saying she didn't have faith. I am sure right now that you feel as I did how horrible this is that people did that to her. Maybe we don't actually walk out with our feet but in our mind we don't even bother to pray. Instead we come up with all sorts of reasons and excuses why that person has that sickness and why they won't be healed. Let me warn you there is no faith in that at all. But that is where your actual "faith?" is, and when you need faith for yourself that is what is going to come up and not faith at all. We must rid ourselves of everything that says God won't or can't and get to real faith.

What that pastor's wife really needed in that moment was for people to come alongside her and encourage her to fight the good fight of faith. Despite the pain of abandonment and betrayal, she continued to fight and win. Today she is cancer free!

Hebrews 12:12-13 "So **take a new grip with your tired hands** and strengthen your weak knees. Mark out a straight path for your feet so that those who are weak and lame will not fall but become strong."NLT

Isaiah 35:3-6 "**Encourage the exhausted** and strengthen the feeble. Say to those with anxious heart, "Take courage, fear not." The recompense of God will come, But He will save you" Then the eyes of the blind will be opened and the ears of the deaf will be unstopped. The lame will leap like a deer, and the tongue of the mute will shout for joy."NASB

What if we were brave enough to just simply believe that God will heal everyone who comes to Him? What if we stopped judging and criticizing? What if we refrained from coming up with endless reasons and excuses? What if we just came alongside people encouraging them to fight the good fight of faith?

We just need to believe!
I am healed because of my faith in Jesus and in His compassion for me.

There is a story in Mark 4 where we find Jesus and His disciples at a boat docked on the shore. Jesus tells His disciples that they are going to get into the boat and go to the other side. While crossing the sea, Jesus went to sleep down below. Not a big deal, right? Wrong. As a storm began to brew, and the boat began to rock back and forth, panic arose amongst the disciples. We know how the rest of the story goes: Jesus calmed the storm and they made it to the other side, just like He said they would. Yet in that moment, their faith was small and their fear was large. **So, in those moments when you feel panic surge like electricity through your body, take courage in the fact that Jesus will calm the storm.** The disciples were skilled fishermen, supposedly well trained in storm navigation and relief, yet they still fumbled around the situation, alarmed and distressed enough to wake up their sleeping Teacher. Even more than this, these men were His disciples who walked and talked with Him on a daily basis. They saw miracles happen all the time! Yet, they too spoke fear and doubt in the midst of a storm. Jesus, with His great compassion and love, still calmed the storm and performed the miracle.

Do not allow the enemy to lie to you and encourage you to believe that God will not bring you to the other side. Do not, in your moment of weakness, further allow condemnation to weigh you down. **For anyone looking at the boat, it is easy to belittle the severity of the storm.** It is easy to judge and criticize from a steady shore.

Jesus, in His great compassion for us, will not leave us in what seems to be the most violent of storms. His compassion will perform a miracle, even when we are fighting through thoughts and fears and words of discouragement.

The devil is a liar, but *OUR GOD CANNOT LIE.*

This is Jesus' faith. This is what Jesus' "gut theology" is (red letter, His actual words): *Matthew 6:10* "Your will be done on earth as it is in heaven."NKJV
There is no sickness, disease, pain or tears in heaven. That is God's same will on the earth.

Hebrews 11:6 "It is impossible to please God without faith. Anyone who wants to come to Him must believe that God exists and that He rewards those who sincerely seek Him."NLT

Keep fighting the good fight my friend! It is always God's will to heal you.

I know you've told yourself so many reasons why God won't heal you. **Let me give you 15 reasons right now why He will heal you:**

1. He's the same yesterday today and forever. *Hebrews 13:8*
2. He's no respecter of persons. *Acts 10:34*
3. He even healed the Greek woman's daughter who was outside of the Israelites covenant rights. *Mark 7:24-30*
4. God cannot lie. *Hebrews 6:18*

5. His word accomplishes what it was sent to do. *Isaiah 55:11*
6. He **loves** you. *Romans 8:37-39*
7. It's His will be done on earth like it is in heaven. *Matthew 6:10-11*
8. It is ALWAYS His will to heal. *Acts 10:38*
9. It's His character and nature. *Matthew 9:35*
10. Whatever you ask in prayer, believing, you will receive. *Matthew 21:22*
11. The Word heals. *Matthew 8:5-13*
12. You have been given authority to heal every kind of disease and illness. *Matthew 10:1*
13. God is merciful. *Psalm 145:8*
14. It's your benefit right. *Psalm 103:2-3*
15. He paid the ultimate price for it! Of course He wants you to have it! *1 Peter 2:24*

GOD CANNOT LIE

This truth was a game changer for me. It became my daily, out-loud declaration. It was what I purposed to intentionally trust more than anything thing else.

"GOD CANNOT LIE"

Hebrews 10:35-36 "Therefore do not cast away your confidence, which has great reward. For you have need of endurance, so that after you have done the will of God, you may receive the promise."NKJV

Ephesians 6:14 "Having done all to stand. Stand therefore, having **girded your waist with truth**."NKJV

My symptoms did not go away immediately, as with some miracles that I had seen before. I knew, though, that God's Word says that He cannot lie. So I **"girded"** myself with that truth. When a tree is girded, a strip (much like a belt) is taken out, all the way around it. It does not immediately die, it may even look, very much, alive. But, if it has been **girded**, it has to die. It is an inevitable eventuality, just like my symptoms were.

Psalm 28:7 "The Lord is my strength and shield. I trust him with all my heart. He helps me, and my heart is filled with joy. I burst out in songs of thanksgiving."NLT

Luke 1:37 "**For with God nothing will be impossible.**"NKJV

Mark 11:22 "Then Jesus said to the disciples, "**Have faith in God**."NLT

John 6:63 "It is the Spirit who gives life; the flesh profits nothing. The words that I speak to you are spirit, and they are life."NKJV

Revelation 12:11 " And they overcame him by the blood of the Lamb and by the word of their testimony."NKJV

Psalm 138:2 "You have magnified your Word above your name."NKJV

Jeremiah 1:12 "Then the LORD said to me, "You have seen well, for I am [actively] watching over My word to fulfill it."AMP

Nothing will build your faith as quickly as confession. Faith comes by hearing the Word of God:

- Confess it in your heart first.
- Confess it out loud in your room.
- Say it over and over again.
- Say it until your spirit and your words agree.

- Say it until your whole being swings into harmony and into line with the Word of God.

"GOD CANNOT LIE"

Psalms 91:2-4 "This I declare about the LORD: He alone is my refuge, my place of safety; he is my God, and I trust him. For he will rescue you from every trap and protect you from deadly disease. He will cover you with his feathers. He will shelter you with his wings. His faithful promises are your armor and protection."NLT

Psalms 107:20 "He sent His word and healed them, And delivered them from their destructions."NKJV

"GOD CANNOT LIE"

2 Chronicles 30:18-20 "Hezekiah prayed for them, saying, "May the good LORD provide atonement for everyone who prepares his heart to seek God, the LORD God of his fathers, though he is not cleansed according to the purification of the sanctuary." And the LORD listened to Hezekiah and healed the people."NKJV

Galatians 3:13-14 "Christ has redeemed us from the curse of the law, having become a curse for us (for it is written, "Cursed is everyone who hangs on a tree"), that the blessing of Abraham might come upon the Gentiles in Christ Jesus, that we might receive the promise of the Spirit through faith."NKJV

Exodus 23:25-26 "So you shall serve the LORD your God, and He will bless your bread and your water. And I will take sickness away from the midst of you…I will fulfill the number of your days."NKJV

"GOD CANNOT LIE"

James 5:14-16 "Is anyone among you sick? Let him call for the elders of the church, and let them pray over him, anointing him with oil in the name of the Lord. And the prayer of faith will save the sick, and the Lord will raise him up. And if he has committed sins, he will be forgiven. Confess your trespasses to one another, and pray for one another, that you may be healed. The effective, fervent prayer of a righteous man avails much."NKJV

Luke 4:40 "When the sun was setting, all those who had ANY that were sick with various diseases brought them to Him; and He laid His hands on every one of them and healed them." NKJV

Matthew 4:23-24 " And Jesus went about all Galilee, teaching in their synagogues, preaching the gospel of the kingdom, and healing all kinds of sickness and all kinds of disease among the people. Then His fame went throughout all Syria; and they brought to Him all sick people who were afflicted with various diseases and torments, and those who were demon-possessed, epileptics, and paralytics; and **He healed them**."NKJV

Matthew 9:35 "Then Jesus went about all the cities and villages, teaching in their synagogues, preaching the gospel of the kingdom, and **healing every sickness and every disease among the people**."NKJV

Matthew 10:1 "And when He had called His twelve disciples to Him, **He gave them power over unclean spirits, to cast them out, and to heal all kinds of sickness and all kinds of disease.**"NKJV

Matthew 12:15 "But when Jesus knew it, He withdrew from there. And great multitudes followed Him, and **He healed them all**."NKJV

Matthew 14:35-36 "And when the men of that place recognized Him, they sent out into all that surrounding region, brought to Him all who were sick, and begged Him that they might only touch the hem of His garment. And as many as touched it were made perfectly well."NKJV

Luke 6:17,19 "And He came down with them and stood on a level place with a crowd of His disciples and a great multitude of people from all Judea and Jerusalem, and from the seacoast of Tyre and Sidon, who came to hear Him and be healed of their diseases, and the whole multitude sought to touch Him, for power went out from Him and healed them all." NKJV

John 14:12-14 "Most assuredly, I say to you, he who believes in Me, the works that I do he will do also; and greater works than these he will do, because I go to My Father. And whatever you ask in My name, that I will do, that the Father may be glorified in the Son. If you ask anything in My name, I will do it."NKJV

Jeremiah 23:29 "Is not My word like a fire?" says the LORD, "And like a hammer that breaks the rock in pieces?"NKJV

"GOD CANNOT LIE"

Hebrews 2:14 "Since then the children are sharers in flesh and blood, he also himself in like manner partook of the same; that through death he might BRING TO NOUGHT him that had the power of death, that is, the devil." ASV *emphasis mine*

Hebrews 11:1 "Faith is the confidence that what we hope for will actually happen; it gives us assurance about things we cannot see."NLT

2 Corinthians 1:20 "For all the promises of God in Him are Yes, and in Him Amen, to the glory of God through us."NLT

1 John 3:8 "**The Son of God came to destroy the works of the devil.**"NLT

Psalm 145:8-9 "The Lord is merciful and compassionate, slow to get angry and filled with unfailing love.The Lord is good to everyone. He showers compassion on all his creation."NLT

Psalms 25:10 "The LORD leads with unfailing love and faithfulness all who keep his covenant and obey his demands."NLT

Acts 28:9 **"Then all the other sick people on the island came and were healed."**NLT

Isaiah 53:4-5 "Yet it was our weaknesses He carried; it was our sorrows that weighed Him down. And we thought His troubles were a punishment from God, a punishment for His own sins! But He was pierced for our rebellion, crushed for our sins. He was beaten so we could be whole. **He was whipped so we could be healed.**"NLT

Matthew 8:17 "This fulfilled the word of the Lord through the prophet Isaiah, who said, 'He took our sicknesses and removed our diseases.'"NLT

"GOD CANNOT LIE"

Deuteronomy 7:9 "Understand, therefore, that the LORD your God is indeed God. He is the faithful God who keeps his covenant for a thousand generations and lavishes his unfailing love on those who love him and obey his commands."NLT

Mark 16:17-18 "These miraculous signs will accompany those who believe: They will cast out demons in My name, and they will speak in new languages. They will be able to handle snakes with safety, and if they drink anything poisonous, it won't hurt them. They will be able to place their hands on the sick, and they will be healed."NLT

1 Thessalonians 2:13 "For this reason we also thank God without ceasing, because when you received the word of God which you heard from us, you welcomed it not as the word of men, but as it is in truth, the word of God, which also effectively works in you who believe."NKJV

James 4:7 "Therefore submit to God. **Resist the devil and he will flee from you.**"NKJV

2 Corinthians 10:5 "We are destroying sophisticated arguments and every exalted and proud thing that sets itself up against the [true] knowledge of God, and we are taking every thought and purpose captive to the obedience of Christ." AMP

Proverbs 3:7-8 "Do not be wise in your own eyes; **Fear the LORD** [with reverent awe and obedience] and turn [entirely] away from evil. **It will be health to your body** [your marrow, your nerves, your sinews, your muscles--all your inner parts] And refreshment (physical well-being) to your bones." AMP

Psalm 84:11 "For the LORD God is a sun and shield; The LORD bestows grace and favor and honor; **No good thing will He withhold from those who walk uprightly.**" AMP

Psalm 91:14 "Because he set his love on Me, therefore I will save him; I will set him [securely] on high, because he knows My name [he confidently trusts and relies on Me, knowing I will never abandon him, no, never]." AMP

2 Chronicles 16:9 "The eyes of the LORD search the whole earth in order to strengthen those whose hearts are fully committed to him." NLT

Romans 8:11 "The Spirit of God, who raised Jesus from the dead, lives in you. And just as God raised Christ Jesus from the dead, he will give life to your mortal bodies by this same Spirit living within you."NLT

"GOD CANNOT LIE"

John 4:50 "Then Jesus told him, 'Go back home. Your son will live!' And the man believed what Jesus said and started home."NLT

Titus 1:1-2 "This letter is from Paul, a slave of God and an apostle of Jesus Christ. I have been sent to proclaim faith to those God has chosen and to teach them to know the truth that shows them how to live godly lives. This truth gives them confidence that they have eternal life, which God—who does not lie—promised them before the world began."NLT

Numbers 23:19 "God is not a man, so He does not lie. He is not human, so He does not change His mind. Has he ever spoken and failed to act? Has He ever promised and not carried it through?"NLT

1 Samuel 15:29 "And He who is the Glory of Israel will not lie, nor will He change His mind, for He is not human that He should change His mind!"NLT

Hebrews 6:17-20 "God also bound himself with an oath, so that those who received the promise could be perfectly sure that He would never change His mind. So God has given both His promise and His oath. These two things are unchangeable because it is impossible for God to lie. Therefore, we who have fled to Him for refuge can have great confidence as we hold to the hope that lies before us. This hope is a strong and trustworthy anchor for our souls. It leads us through the curtain into God's inner sanctuary. Jesus has already gone in there for us. He has become our eternal High Priest in the order of Melchizedek."NLT

God's Word is His Will & Testament

Until we know what the will of God is and believe that it is for us, we are living a substandard life. There are lists of benefits in the Word of God, but until we believe and receive, they remain just words on paper.

The word "testament" is used when referring to a person's will. Legally speaking, it is called the "last will and testament" and is a legal document by which the person who died has expressed in detail exactly how everything of theirs is to be distributed.

Here is your inheritance - God's will & testament to you:

Psalms 103:2-5 "**Bless the LORD**, O my soul, And forget not all His benefits: Who forgives all your iniquities, **Who heals all your diseases**, Who redeems your life from destruction, Who crowns you with lovingkindness and tender mercies, Who satisfies your mouth with good things, So that your youth is renewed like the eagle's."NKJV

Proverbs 4:20-22 "My son, give attention to my words; incline your ear to my sayings. Do not let them depart from your sight; keep them in the midst of your heart. For they are life to those who find them and health to all their body."NASB

1 John 5:14 "This is the confidence which we have before Him, that, **if we ask anything according to His will, He hears us**."NASB

Psalms 119:89-90 "Forever, O LORD, Your word is settled in heaven.Your faithfulness endures to all generations; You established the earth, and it abides."NKJV

Hebrews 13:8 "**Jesus Christ is the same yesterday, today, and forever.**"NKJV

One of the most wonderful things about God's Word - our truth - is that it never changes. **It is neither altered by its environment nor affected by circumstances**. Truth, however, is either activated or deactivated by its reception.

God's will and testament for us is life, and it is life to the absolute fullest.

It is God's will to heal you. He is no respecter of persons. He is the same yesterday, today and forever.

"GOD CANNOT LIE"

WAVERING FAITH OR FIGHTING THE GOOD FIGHT?

Here I am, in the middle of the biggest fight of my life, doing all I can to stand on God's Word but still, in comes the devil whispering in my ear; "It is written…do not waver, such people should not expect to receive anything from the Lord…you are wavering…you are going to die."

The devil is the father of lies, yet he still left me feeling like I was wavering, even though I was not, and he was the one who planted the thought there. Can you see what I see? This is all a set up.

You see, even though my heart is fixed and I know I am healed; even though I have declared it with my mouth over and over and my mind has been made up, this does not mean the devil will stop setting us up to fail, whispering lies in our ears and leaving us feeling completely condemned. It also does not mean that people will not say things contrary to our declaration, or that we will not have flashes of fear that try to grip us. These things are going to happen. What we need to recognize is that just because they do, does not mean that we are wavering in our faith and will not receive our healing from the Lord.

1 Timothy 6:12 tells us to "fight the good fight of faith." A fight is truly only a fight when there are two opposing sides. That simply means that the good fight of faith has got to have an enemy in order to be referred to as a fight. The wrong or negative thoughts in your head are not a sign of unsteadiness, they are just a sign of a fight. It is what we do with the wrong or negative thoughts that will make or break us at the end of the day.

So, do not allow yourself to get confused or tripped up with real wavering versus fighting the good fight of faith. Real wavering would be to succumb to every thought of doubt and fear; it is when you start to believe the lies, and then you start to accept them. But, if your heart is fixed on faith and you are holding up the Word of God above all else, then you, my friend, are not wavering. **You are fighting**.

I almost fell for this lie from the devil, too, that because I wrestled in my thoughts, that meant I was wavering and should not expect anything from God. But I knew that **God cannot lie**. I did not change my confession to myself, to people around me, or to the doctors - my faith was fixed! I was fighting the good fight. The devil could not have my faith; there was no way that I was falling for his lies.

I do not know where you are, or what lies are being thrown in your direction, but what I do know is that it is all a set up, and you can fix your heart on faith. Take those thoughts captive and do not waver. You will receive what you believe.

Maybe you are reading this, but you believe that you do not have big enough, or strong enough, faith. There is a passage in the book of Proverbs that I absolutely love, it says: "Ants - they are not strong, but they store up food all summer…and that we are to consider (look at the ant and learn from them)." (Proverbs 30:25, 6:6 AMPC)

You do not have to be "strong" to win.

Do not let go of your faith because of the devil's set up. James 4:7 tells us to "Resist the devil and he will flee." That is awesome!

Faith is not faith at all, if you have to see it first.

Hebrews 11:1,3 "Faith is the confidence that what we hope for will actually happen; **it gives us assurance about things we cannot see**. By faith we understand that the entire universe was formed at God's command, that what we now see did not come from anything that can be seen."NLT

2 Corinthians 5:7 "For we live by believing and not by seeing."NLT

Gravity is so interesting. We never ever think about it, but we believe in it every single day and act in faith that it will work, not for any other reason but the fact that we have always been able to count on it in the past. How much more should we have faith in our supernatural God, who created all things with the words of His mouth.

I totally understand that there is a temptation to forget what *is* working and focus on what is not working. But the fact remains - gravity is still working. There is solid ground under your feet. **Focus on what is working even if you cannot see it, because, even though you can't see it, it is working**.

Jesus is the same yesterday, today and forever. God cannot lie and His Word goes on forever, just like He said:

"let there be light"
and there was, and
there is still light today.

His spoken Word will sustain and go throughout all of eternity, never fading away.

The Bible does not say anything about faith coming by what you see, or what you feel. It says very simply that, "Faith cometh by hearing, and hearing by the word of God." (Romans 10:17). Faith is believing the Word of God before you can see or feel a natural manifestation of it.

Romans 4:18-24 "Even when there was no reason for hope, Abraham kept hoping—believing that he would become the father of many nations. For God had said to him, "That's how many descendants you will have!" And Abraham's faith did not weaken, even though, at about 100 years of age, he figured his body was as good as dead—and so was Sarah's womb. Abraham never wavered in believing God's promise. In fact, his faith grew stronger, and in this he brought glory to God. He was fully convinced that God is able to do whatever he promises. And because of Abraham's faith, God counted him as righteous. And when God counted him as righteous, it wasn't just for Abraham's benefit. It was recorded for our benefit, too, assuring us that God will also count us as righteous if we believe in him, the one who raised Jesus our Lord from the dead."NLT

Hebrews 10:23 "Let us hold tightly without wavering to the hope we affirm, for God can be trusted to keep his promise." NLT

Again, **as long as gravity is working, as long as the sun is setting and still rising, you can count on God that His promises are true, because He is working**. His supernatural power of creation is still working. Trust in His promises even when you cannot see them, because they are yes and amen and true for every single person.

Psalm 93:1, 5 "The world is firmly established, it cannot be moved. Your precepts are fully confirmed and completely reliable." AMP

On all of this I stand in faith. I know and do not waver: God cannot lie, and His power is evidenced all around me in creation still today. Of this truth, I do not even question or think of wavering. I am not questioning gravity with every step I take. No, I just know that it is working. I do not question the earth's rotation or the setting and rising of the sun. No, I just know that it is happening. So, I really don't question the power of God, I just believe confidently that the power of God is working through all of creation, **including me**.

Romans 12:3 "God hath dealt to each man a measure of faith." ASV

Take courage. Everyone has a measure of faith-
everyone.

CHARACTER AND NATURE OF GOD

Not of yourself lest anyone should boast
Ephesians 2:8-9, Psalms 115:1

We have to trust that no matter what we are facing, GOD WILL MAKE A WAY! It is not only His Word, but it is also His will, His nature, and His character. We see God making a way in impossible situations all throughout His awesome Word. He even makes a way for advancement, promotion, and blessing. Untroubled and undisturbed blessing is our portion! So trust today that no matter what you are believing for - OUR GOD WILL MAKE A WAY. Expect it!

Isaiah 43:16, 19 "Thus says the Lord, Who MAKES a way through the sea and a path through the mighty waters, Behold, I will do something new, Now it will spring forth; Will you not be aware of it? I will even MAKE a roadway in the wilderness, rivers in the desert."NKJV

"God WILL make a way." Let this be your response to yourself and everyone else you encounter today.

Luke 8:48 "He said to her, 'Daughter, your faith [your personal trust and confidence in Me] has made you well. Go in peace (untroubled, undisturbed well-being).'" AMP

Ephesians 3:20 "Now all glory to God, who is able, through his mighty power at work within us, to accomplish infinitely more than we might ask or think." NLT

Deuteronomy 30:19 "Today I have given you the choice between life and death, between blessings and curses. Now I call on heaven and earth to witness the choice you make. Oh, that you would choose life, so that you and your descendants might live!" NLT

2 Peter 1:3 "By his divine power the Lord has given us everything we need for life and godliness." NLT

Now, maybe as you are sitting there, you do not disagree with what I am saying, but there is still a small part of you saying:

"But you do not really understand my situation."
"You do not understand where I am at."
"In my life, I have always gotten the short end of the stick."
"I always get the raw end of the deal."
"If you were only in my situation, you would not say that."
"I've been diagnosed with this sickness."
"I simply do not have the finances I need or the means to get it."
"I do not have any control over what is happening to me."

I want you to be assured that I am sensitive to what you are feeling. I have even had some of those thoughts myself. But **what really counts at the end of the day is what His Word says**. My Bible tells me that my God is no respecter of persons and, so, what He has done for me, He will do for you! Your case is not exempt from His will and testament.

Psalm 103:2-5 "Bless the LORD, O my soul, and forget not all his benefits:
Who forgiveth all thine iniquities; who healeth all thy diseases;
Who redeemeth thy life from destruction; who crowneth thee with lovingkindness and tender mercies;
Who satisfieth thy mouth with good *things; so that* thy youth is renewed like the eagle's."KJV

1 Corinthians 1:17 "For Christ sent me not to baptize, but to preach the gospel: not with wisdom of words, lest the cross of Christ should be made of none effect" KJV

God is all powerful, and that overwhelming fact has nothing to do with you or me, or else we would be able to receive the glory for His miracle. It is all about God. It is not about what "we did right," or how we are "better" than the other person. It is God's will that not one of His precious children be sick or have disease. He is a miracle worker who "is the same yesterday, today, and forever!" (Hebrews 13:8) It is His character and nature.

Jesus delivered and healed the demoniac, who was pure evil, filled with the legions of demons. Was he healed because he did everything right? Was it because he believed that he was a good person and did everything that he was "supposed" to do?

No, it is simply because the almighty power of God does miracles so great.

Nothing can stand at the name of Jesus. Everything must bow. His name is above all. Because He paid the ultimate price by dying for us on the cross, both the power of sin and sickness were destroyed. We often only remember to look at the sin portion of salvation, while the other half is busy killing both us and our loved ones. Just like sin, Jesus wills that none be sick. He paid the full price. Both have got nothing to do with our own efforts, and everything to do with His goodness.

I am alive today simply because of my faith in the all-powerful, miracle-working, compassionate God - not because of anything I can do, lest I should boast.

Ephesians 2:8-9 "For it is by grace [God's remarkable compassion and favor drawing you to Christ] that you have been saved [actually delivered from judgment and given eternal life] through faith. And this [salvation] is not of yourselves [not through your own effort], but it is the [undeserved, gracious] gift of God; not as a result of [your] works [nor your attempts to keep the Law], so that no one will [be able to] boast or take credit in any way [for his salvation]." AMP

When God hangs around it's not long before something good's going to happen. It's His character and nature. #Linger

Our faith must become an unwavering eventuality.

Humans are funny when it comes to healing. We think our dos-and-don'ts are worth so much when in all actuality they just damage our faith. I like how my friend Susan Carberry describes human behavior when it comes to healing; "It is like the last 9 yards of a touchdown. It plays out. But you are watching yesterday's game, you know the touchdown already was achieved. But still, as humans, we get caught up in the tension and drama of the play...as it plays out."

If God did it for one, He will do it for all.

Only keep believing, for God cannot lie. The cross of Christ and the purchased victory it achieved is effective for everyone. Just like you accept the cross was for your sins, the same way accept that is was also to heal your body. Compassion and healing are the very character and nature of the amazing God that we serve.

Today my battle feels like only a bad dream I once had. But, I know the reality of it, and that every day and every breath I get to breathe is a gift from God.

God cannot lie, my friend. Keep fighting the good fight for your faith! I know first-hand the feelings and challenges of having done all, to stand, but you MUST keep standing. You may need to take a new grip with your tired hands, but hold on. **It's my prayer for you that, as you read these pages, the powerful, sharp, life-giving Word of God will accomplish what it is sent to do.** It is my hope for you that my very real and transparent testimony encourages you, causes you to sift through your doubts and fears, and lifts your faith. Now, let's glorify God together!

Other Resources By Rhonda Spencer

NO MORE HURT

NO MORE HURT WORKBOOK

RhondaJSpencer.com

EmpoweringPastorsWives.com

Made in the USA
Lexington, KY
21 June 2018